DISCOVER THE
TAROT

DISCOVER THE
TAROT

SHIRLEY WALLIS

BLANDFORD

First published in the UK 1991 by Blandford
Villiers House, 41/47 Strand, London WC2N 5JE

A Cassell Imprint

British Library Cataloguing in Publication Data

Wallis, Shirley
  Discover the tarot
  1. Tarot cards
  I. Title
  133.32424

  ISBN 0–7137–2305–X

Typeset in 11 on 11½ point ITC Garamond Light by
Columns Design and Production Services Ltd, Reading.

Printed and bound in Great Britain by
Mackays of Chatham PLC

Dedication

To my Father and Mother with love.

Acknowledgements

Special thanks to my daughter Annalisa for invaluable help in typing the manuscript. Thanks to my son Alex and daughter Kate for their co-operation, enthusiasm and patience.

Sincere gratitude to my dear friends Patrick, Angela and Pat for inspiration and discussion, to the illustrator Anna Powell for her flair and originality and to all those friends and clients who have joined with me in the Journey.

Thanks and appreciation to AGM AGMÜLLER of Switzerland for granting permission to reproduce line drawings of the Greater Arcana from their 1JJ Tarot pack. © 1990 AgMüller, Switzerland. Distributed in the UK by Element Books Ltd., and David Westnedge Ltd., London. Line drawings of cards by Mike Shoebridge.

THE FOOL

CONTENTS

INTRODUCTION   9

Chapter 1: THE TAROT PACK OF CARDS   11

Chapter 2: GETTING STARTED   18

Chapter 3: EXAMPLES OF READINGS   25

Chapter 4: THE GREATER ARCANA   42
            Pictures and Meanings

Chapter 5: THE LESSER ARCANA   100
            Meanings

INDEX   123

INTRODUCTION

This book is aimed at anyone who wants to find out about the Tarot or begin to use it; for anyone who wants to begin again for various reasons; and for anyone who already uses it but may wish to see it in a new light. We are all beginners and searchers.

The Tarot has its origins back in the mists of time and, because of the mystery surrounding its source, we must first of all realise that we are dealing with much more than a large pack of unusual-looking cards. Secondly, any form of divination and symbolism must be respected for the art that it represents, and with the Tarot there is an ancient wisdom as well as traditions attached to it. This book acts as an introduction to a new adventure with some guidelines on how to play this game of discovery: it is then up to us how we use this pictorial wisdom.

These are essentially my own ways of using the cards based upon their traditions and how you can relate to both the mind and the feelings, thus achieving insight by the use of Tarot cards.

Chapter 1

THE TAROT PACK
OF CARDS

There are many different packs of cards from which to choose, each illustrated in their own ways, but they all follow the same tradition and wisdom as it has evolved through the ages. You should choose a pack with which you feel 'comfortable', perhaps preferring one type of illustration to another.

The Tarot is made up of 78 cards, of which 22 are known as the **Greater Arcana** and the remaining 56 cards are called the **Lesser Arcana**.

THE GREATER ARCANA
(or Major Arcana)

These 22 cards are numbered 1–21, with an un-numbered card — The Fool — completing this section of the pack. These are sometimes marked with Roman numerals which are included in the cards illustrated on pp. 42–99. You can use them independently from the Lesser Arcana (the remaining 56 cards), if you wish.

These cards are regarded as representing stages in the quest for knowledge, enlightenment and understanding in our journey through life. The psychological meaning of the cards is probably their most important aspect, but each card by its picture and symbolism can still give answers on any level according to the type of question posed.

This section provides the framework of the Tarot, so practise with these 22 cards first and become familiar with the pictures and let the symbolism speak to you. When you have read through this Chapter, turn to the illustrations and explanations of the cards on page 42 to give yourself an initial idea of the interpretations.

THE LESSER ARCANA
(or Minor Arcana)

These 56 cards represent different levels of human existence and awareness of life in both material and spiritual ways. These levels are described by the four suits (as in ordinary playing cards), which are called BATONS (sometimes called Wands, Sceptres), COINS, SWORDS and CUPS (Chalices). The names may vary slightly according to which make of pack you use, but the meanings are exactly the same.

Each suit contains:

KING (ROI)
QUEEN (REINE)
KNIGHT (CAVALIER or CHEVALIER)
KNAVE (VALET or PAGE)

These 16 COURT cards represent people when they appear in a layout or reading using the whole pack, e.g. A person brings an influence which will have some significance in any future actions you may take. (The King of Coins could be your Bank Manager!) The remaining 40 cards are numbered 1 (ACE) to 10 for each of the suits. So the Lesser Arcana has 56 cards divided into four suits, Batons, Coins, Swords and Cups starting with the King, Queen, Knight, Knave, 1 (ACE) through to 10. These four suits describe human existence by using the four elements Fire, Earth, Air and Water because these are linked to the four suits as follows:

BATONS: Fire

This suit represents the exercise of the will: taking action with ideas, using the intellect with inspiration. Generally, enterprise and progress with endeavours.

Batons Court cards often refer to persons in the working class bracket: labourers, factory workers.

COINS: Earth

This suit represents material/financial wealth, comfort, security, stability and the world of business and commerce.

Coins Court cards refer to people in business: managers, accountants, financiers and merchants.

SWORDS: Air

The suit of Swords is concerned with negotiations and agreements, discussion and debate. The desire to establish order, compete and make contracts — for good or ill.

Swords Court cards describe persons in authority: executives, leaders, and the upper classes.

CUPS: Water

This suit is concerned with emotional matters: love, feelings, creative pursuits and a general feeling of happiness.

Cups Court cards describe two types of people: Persons in religious or philosophical groups, the clergy; and those in show business or entertainment who bring happiness to others or who are engaged in any cultural activities.

READING THE CARDS

We can view the cards in three ways:

1. As symbolising immediate concerns and questions regarding everyday life.
2. As representing the 'quest' of the unconscious part of us — the soul's journey through human existence or life, where the 22 cards of the Greater Arcana represent the stages and responsibilities each of the cards illustrate.
3. By taking both of the above levels, moulding them into a 'whole' approach because we are ready to accept and understand that life is a journey and we can use the cards as signposts to direct us, taking into account that what we desire immediately may not be what is really best for us in developing and refining all our qualities.

Naturally, the last, combined approach is the one to aim for (No 3), but by starting with No 1 and learning how the basic interpretations unfold, you will see how the symbolism of the cards answers your questions.

COMPOSING THE QUESTION

So what sort of questions can be asked? First of all, you must always keep in mind what you *really* want to know to allow the cards to give you the most helpful answer.

If you ask questions like: 'Will I marry soon?' or 'Shall

I win the Pools?' or 'Will I pass my driving test?' you will find it difficult to interpret the meanings of the cards, simply because the questions are demanding a Yes or No answer. True, that is what you may desire, but the cards reply through a sequence according to how you lay them out, so what you must try to do is (a) think carefully and clarify in your mind what you *really* want to know, and then (b) ask the kind of question which allows the cards to give you a sequence which, through each of the individual cards' meanings, builds up the answer.

For example, if you want to know if you'll pass your driving test, your first question could be: 'What are the circumstances like at the time of my driving test?' The cards will then reveal, through the layout you have used, a sequence of indications about the prevailing circumstances. If difficulties are revealed, then you will be prepared to behave carefully and positively in the face of the circumstances. You will have control of the matter in hand and should attempt to turn it to your advantage. Then, if you pass your driving test, you will experience more of an 'in-depth' sense of achievement which will give you more confidence and an improved way of accepting this new responsibility. If you don't pass your test this time, you will learn that you weren't ready to take on this responsibility just yet. Hopefully, you will realise that more work must be done on your part so that outside influences cannot deter you from your goal.

This type of question allows the cards to *help* you, so the layout can be simple enough to show you what you can expect, but also comprehensive enough to give you background information for the past, present and future. What I am encouraging you to do, before you plunge into laying out the cards, is to *think first*. Allow a little time to get in 'tune' with yourself and your cards. You should be the only person who handles them except for when your questioner shuffles and cuts them prior to a reading, so keep the cards in a safe place. Tradition has it that they should be wrapped in a piece of dark silk, perhaps black or purple. You might like to find a special container for them too.

THE ENERGY AT PLAY

Some years ago, the Cornish writer, Michael Williams interviewed me and asked: 'How can a thing like Tarot cards really help to map out a person's future. Isn't the fall of the cards all luck or chance?' I replied: 'Tarot cards are an immediate expression of the energies at play *today*. Throw them again tomorrow and possibly you will find a different scene, though there would be links. It all depends on your question. You do need signposts or guidelines in order to make some sort of judgement, and this is why I use the Tarot'. Notice I said '. . . the energies at play today'. There is energy everywhere — it never stops moving. We ourselves can be viewed as having our own 'force field'. Some people have an abundance of physical energy which they express in sports or games or dancing. Others have more mental energy which they express through writing or speech. It is this mental energy which we use, of course, when consulting the Tarot cards.

BRAIN POWER

The brain has two hemispheres which see the world in different ways. Scientific research has been exploring these two halves of the brain for many years. It has been found that the left side specialises in verbal and analytical thought, and the right side specialises in the understanding of patterns and intuition. Basically speaking, the left side codes memory in linguistic description, while the right codes memory in images.

Our scientific-based mode of living has depended upon us increasing and developing methods of analysing

— which is characteristic of the left-hand hemisphere of the brain. This has led to a general neglect of the right-hand hemisphere and therefore we should hardly be surprised if its functioning seems elusive or even mysterious. We have got out of the habit of listening to this right-hand, intuitive half of the brain, or view those people who do as being slightly 'weird'.

A well-balanced person operates either parts of the brain according to the task in hand, or uses them in conjunction with one another. By using Tarot cards, we are developing this right-hand intuitive response to symbols and images. We must allow this function to operate freely as well as the left-hand analytical, reasoning response. Your intuition is a wonderful part of you. It is the 'knowing' about something which you can't really explain. This is why the symbolism of the Tarot cards is important and why it still survives after many centuries.

Chapter 2

GETTING STARTED

You are called the Diviner and your client is the Questioner. Sit opposite each other at a table with a good, clean surface. You may find it helpful to face the East if possible. Take out the cards from their wrapping and decide whether you are going to use just the 22 cards of the Greater (or Major) Arcana or the whole pack of 78. To begin with, it's a good idea to use the Greater Arcana only and get to know them first, so set aside the 56 Lesser (or Minor) cards for the present.

THE 7-CARD SPREAD

Shuffle the cards yourself and ask your client what his or her question is. Think quietly about it and then pass the cards to the Questioner asking him to shuffle the cards, stating the question out loud as he does so. Ask him to place the pack, *face down* on the table and cut the cards while thinking about the question; so now there are two piles. Take the pile which was newly exposed and place on top of the other so you are back to one pile. You are now ready to lay out the cards.

From the top, lay out the seven cards *face up* in the following order and pattern: This is what they represent:

Card No 1: The Questioner (this will be your client)
Card No 2: Distant Past
Card No 3: Immediate Past

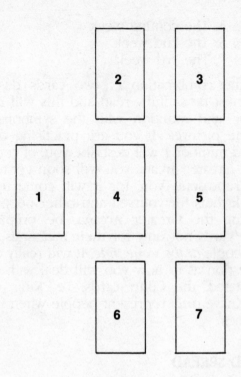

THE 7-CARD SPREAD

Card No 4: Present Influences or Obstacles
Card No 5: Present Outlook
Card No 6: Future Influences
Card No 7: Final Result

Look up the meanings for the cards displayed starting with 1 through to the Final Result, card number 7. You should notice that cards which come out reversed (upside down), generally have a weakening effect wherever they are positioned. You can use this simple spread for any questions, but also as a guide for the immediate 3 weeks ahead thus:

Card No 1: The Questioner

Card Nos 2 & 3: The coming week
Card Nos 4 & 5: The 2nd week
Card Nos 6 & 7: The 3rd week

Obviously, the combination of two cards describing each week must be skilfully read and this will develop your 'feeling' and intuition with the symbolism displayed by the pictures. If you are practising on your own, the card number 1 will describe you, of course, so by using the Greater Arcana you will soon get to know which card represents you, for it will come up quite regularly in layouts for yourself and other people.

When using the Greater Arcana, be prepared to interpret the cards not only for their meanings but for describing people *at the same time*. It will really depend on your question as to how you will deal with this. As previously stated, the Court cards, i.e. King, Queen, Knight and Knave *only* represent people when you use the whole pack.

THE 12-CARD SPREAD

Don't feel inhibited when using a spread — develop your own methods by increasing the number of cards you use, or eventually, create your own type of layouts. For example, you could increase the number of weeks that you look at in the future. However, for the purposes of this book we shall keep to 7 or 12-card spreads. This time, let us use the whole pack of 78 cards:

1. Take out the Greater (Major) Arcana of 22 cards, shuffle them and set them on the table face down.
2. Shuffle the remaining 56 cards of the Lesser (Minor) Arcana, while your Questioner states his question out loud. Place them on the table face down.
3. Ask your Questioner to shuffle the 56 Lesser Arcana pack, then place them face down in a pile.
4. Ask him to cut the cards — while repeating the

question — into two piles (still face down), and then place the newly exposed section on top, thus making one pile.

5. Repeat stages 3 and 4 with the Greater Arcana.
6. Now you have two piles of cards which have been thoroughly shuffled by you both and cut by your Questioner.
7. You, the Diviner now deal 11 cards only from the larger pile, the Lesser Arcana onto the Greater Arcana and shuffle them in, thinking of the question all the time.
8. Ask the Questioner to make a final cut and you are then ready to lay them out in front of you in the following order and pattern:

The first card you place in the centre sets the 'tone' of the reading. You read the cards in an anti-clockwise direction starting with Card No 1 and ending with card No 12.

Each card represents an area of your client's life and is like a horoscope, so if you are familiar with Astrology this is a useful spread for you to develop, but don't worry if you know nothing about it, you can always refer to the following list:

Card No 1: This represents the Questioner, the appearance and attitude.

Card No 2: Material possessions. Money. Attitude to material values, and spiritual values.

Card No 3: Communications. The local community. Education. (If a Court card comes in here it will represent someone with whom you are communicating in some way).

Card No 4: Home base. Domestic situation. Parents or family. Present attitude connected with home. Premises of all kinds.

Card No 5: Personal creativity, sports and pastimes. Children. Romance.

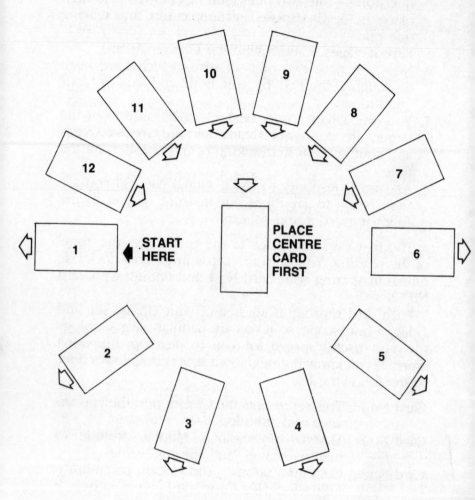

THE CIRCULAR or ASTROL SPREAD

Card No 6: Occupations (jobs). Personal service. Health. Bosses and employees.

Card No 7: Partnerships (marriage or business). Attitude to dialogue/discussion on 'one-to-one' basis.

Card No 8: Other people's resources affecting you (legacies, insurance, taxes etc.). Death. Regenerative influences. Sexual relationships.

Card No 9: Long-distance travel. News from afar. Religion and philosophy. Further education. The Law.

Card No 10: Career or profession. Public image. Social contribution. Parents, their influence, or the attitude of those in authority, toward you.

Card No 11: Friends and Associations. Social values. Hopes and aspirations.

Card No 12: Hidden personal resources and motivations. Secret activities. Inner self.

This spread as you can see is very comprehensive and will meet any requirement no matter what the question or age of your Questioner. You can aim it for the present or future as long as this is stated at the outset. e.g. State the question and then add: 'Now', 'in a month's time', or 'in a year's time' — whatever time your client wishes.

Alternatively, you can use the same spread of 12 cards (with a Centre card for 'tone') to give a general forecast for the coming year, starting with the date of the reading, or do one on New Year's Eve or for someone's birthday, looking at their year ahead.

It is important to note, at this stage, that you can make a 12-card reading using the Greater Arcana or, indeed, a 7-card reading from all 78 cards. Where a number of Greater Arcana cards appear when using the whole pack, these will indicate important points of the reading.

Lastly, don't be tempted to have a mammoth session with the cards on one day. Limit your readings to one each day, and spread the cards three times at the most. The reason for this is that you are using a lot of energy and your 'psyche' gets tired. Other people will always try to persuade you to do 'just one more', but be disciplined, start as you mean to go on and your readings will be all the better as a result.

Chapter 3

EXAMPLES OF READINGS

James is eighteen and will shortly be taking his driving test. He wants to know the outcome because his work is connected with motor vehicles and it will help him to plan his career, especially for the next few months.

I used the Major Arcana and the simple 7-card spread as described in Chapter 2. The question was: *What are the circumstances surrounding James' driving test?* This is how they appeared:

Card No 1: (The Questioner) .... The Hermit (9)
Card No 2: (Distant Past) .... Wheel of Fortune (10)
Card No 3: (Immediate Past) .... Jupiter (5)
Card No 4: (Present Obstacles & Influences)
.... Fortitude (11)
Card No 5: (Present Outlook) .... The World (21)
Card No 6: (Future Influences) .... Judgement (20)
Card No 7: (Final Result) .... The Devil (15)

All of the cards came out *upright*.

Take the above cards from the Greater Arcana and set them out in front of you in the 7-card spread so you can focus your attention on the pictures as we dissect them. Use Chapter 4 for the meanings of the cards as an exercise, for in this way you will soon learn about the cards.

CARD NO 1: THE QUESTIONER

The Hermit symbolises James so we must look at this description, bearing in mind his age. This card shows the Questioner to be quiet and thoughtful, rather withdrawn, and one who has already experienced some of the pitfalls in life, which might make his attitude cautious with regard to the driving test. He is obviously serious and probably feels rather isolated.

CARD NO 2: DISTANT PAST

The Wheel of Fortune (10 in the pack) describes circumstances leading up to the desire to drive a motor vehicle. It is a 'situation' card which bodes well on the whole, but which suggests there have been difficulties in getting the project going and possibly maintaining lessons. (James told me this was true — he was given some lessons as a present to start him off, but later he had financial restrictions). Nevertheless, this was a new beginning.

CARD NO 3: IMMEDIATE PAST

Jupiter (No 5 in the pack) is the Driving Instructor. I arrive at this conclusion because something or somebody contributing to the circumstances surrounding the test is represented by this card. Jupiter has the knowledge — he is a teacher. James has a male instructor.

CARD NO 4: PRESENT OBSTACLES AND INFLUENCES

Fortitude (No 11 in the pack) says that determination is required if James is to succeed (rather obvious, I know), but he is facing a challenge and a risk, probably having some inner doubts and fears (undoubtedly nervous). I warn him that hidden forces are at work — perhaps just his nerves — but there could be something else. Any lack of confidence must be an obstacle anyway.

CARD NO 5: PRESENT OUTLOOK

The World (No 21) in this position looks very encouraging. There is one week to go before the driving test and this card shows that James has achieved what he set out to do, i.e. drive a car competently. We must be careful not to *assume* too much by the appearance of this card — remember, it does represent the *present* outlook.

CARD NO 6: FUTURE INFLUENCES

Judgement (No 20) represents the test itself — the card is a 'situation' card but what sort of influence does it show? It looks very positive with promise of achievement, but we have to remember the question asked was 'What are the *circumstances* surrounding the driving test?' The weather should be very good according to this card, and therefore road conditions will also be good. The Examiner is the judge of the matter and is also symbolised by this card because James has to account to him for all he has achieved so far.

CARD NO 7: FINAL RESULT

The Devil (No 15) weakens the previous card considerably. The circumstances surrounding James' driving test are finalised by showing that hidden influences will be at work. Inner fears (nervousness) can well get the upper hand, so further progress will be blocked if this is the case. I advise James that he stands a very good chance of passing his test, but he must be aware that he will have to work hard at keeping a positive attitude as there are negative influences working. If he feels insecure about any part of the requirement — for instance reversing, or if some unexpected incident occurs — he must try to remain calm and positive.

If this card had been in the Reverse position in the layout, I would have felt extremely confident for him, but I must remind you that it is not a Yes/No set-up for an answer because we have been looking at the *circumstances* surrounding the event. If the cards had been mostly negative in answer to our question, then we would have had a good case for considering a cancellation of the test, thus saving everyone's time and money, but the Tarot on reflection always tries to symbolise as much information and help prior to an event, therefore a person's free will in dealing with difficult symptoms can always be exercised. Practice in defining the symbolism and using your intuition is vital and keeping it simple is quite acceptable. As a Diviner, one must always respect the Questioner and his or her attitude and you should aim to be as positive in reading the cards as you can. Encouragement given to a client or friend is of paramount importance.

One week later, the day of James' driving test dawned. Weather conditions were perfect (Judgement). He said he felt very nervous which was expected. Later that day he reported back to me to say he had not passed and was naturally very disappointed but was man enough to say it was his own fault. However, unforeseen influences were at work — or rather, foreseen by the Tarot.

The driving test went well for the first ten minutes or so, and then, while he was in the middle of the three-point turn, suddenly wailing sirens rent the air and a small motorcade went by, police accompanying a car containing a member of the Royal Family! James said the incident was unexpected enough to throw him right out of gear (so to speak!) and his concentration dwindled from then on culminating in a poor reversing process.

You could call it bad luck, but doubtless the examiner

would be watching for the effect of the 'unexpected' incident upon his examinee.

EXAMPLE 2: THE WEST END PLAY

A character actress of considerable experience and talent was working in London in a West End play. She telephoned me, asking how much longer the play would run. First of all I tried a 12-card circular spread with each of the cards denoting a month from the time of the question, but I found this gave a somewhat confusing result at the beginning of the spread. I left the cards for a day or two until the Monday following the telephone call and sat quietly thinking about the question. My intuition told me to try weeks instead of months for the timing, so I decided to use the Greater Arcana in the 7-card spread, with the Questioner (the actress), as Card No 1 and the following six cards representing the following six weeks.

The question: *How long will the play run in weeks?*

CARD NO 1 (THE QUESTIONER): JUDGEMENT (20) REVERSED

This is the position in which the actress finds herself: something is being judged using the 'situation' meaning described in Chapter 4. The card reversed indicates that facts must be faced and that something is being taken away from her.

CARD NO 2 (THE COMING WEEK) WEEK 1: CHARIOT (7) REVERSED

This indicates that the play's progress is to be halted with no further success — it is not going anywhere. The question is *when*? Let us look at the next card.

CARD NO 3 (WEEK 2): TEMPERANCE (14) UPRIGHT

Read in isolation this card could be indicating some hope, but Temperance does symbolise a pause while discussion and taking everything into account goes on — a resumé, a summing up. The play is obviously coming off, this week or next?

CARD NO 4 (WEEK 3): THE HANGED MAN (12) UPRIGHT

Quite simply, this indicates a suspension of activity — all action has stopped. Nothing is happening. A readjustment is taking place. The play is not running this week! To be certain, let us look at the next cards.

CARD NO 5 (WEEK 4): DEATH (13) REVERSED

The fourth week shows that a fault is prevailing concerning the play. It is fated.

CARD NO 6 (WEEK 5): THE WORLD (21) REVERSED

Failure in achievement, so we know again the play is 'off'.

CARD NO 7 (WEEK 6): THE WHEEL OF FORTUNE (10) REVERSED

Again, failure is denoted by this card which emphasises the previous one.

To recap and answer the actress's question: The card for the first week following the question indicated the play was going nowhere and the end was imminent (Chariot reversed); that set the scene for the second week where Temperance was blending the past, present and future, taking everything into account. The third week showed that all activity was suspended symbolised by The Hanged Man, so we now know the play has ended and can say that it has two more weeks to run from the time of the question, taking into account the last three cards which all indicated failure to back up the decision.

The turning point was slightly confusing with Temperance upright. You could easily read it as causing delay and giving hope initially, but the following card, the Hanged Man told us quite clearly that all was suspended.

That very evening, the actress telephoned after curtain down. I told her the result of the cards: The play has two weeks to run. She then revealed that two weeks notice had been given to the cast at the weekend! Neither of us had thought that the end was so imminent, which was why I originally took the question into a month-by-month reading, and obviously why it couldn't work towards a clear answer.

You can see from this example, how important it is to compose yourself before dealing with the Tarot cards, to ask the right question and try more than one time-scale (weeks, months or years), if you feel it necessary.

EXAMPLE 3: THE INTERVIEW

The most common types of questions that arise in life come about through a variety of reasons — stress, anxiety, sudden changed circumstances, hope for something better or sheer curiosity. For example:

Will I change my job soon?

Will my financial circumstances improve soon?

Shall I go ahead with a project/business venture?

Will I be successful? (Romance, close partnership/a competition/job/business deal etc.).

Will I have a successful interview?

Whatever our age, interviews occur with regularity — perhaps with the headmaster, college principal or for a new job.

Some time ago, a man consulted me regarding his job. John was eager to establish a new career after retiring from a responsible position in the Services. He had tried two different types of employment but was clearly unhappy. An interview was coming up where his administrative abilities would be well suited. Bearing in mind we must ask the right question to give helpful information first, we asked:

What are the influences surrounding the interview?

This time I used the whole pack of 78 cards for a 7-card spread to describe the influences at play for John's interview in order to widen the scope of the reading. This is how they appeared:

CARD NO 1: THE QUESTIONER *WAS* THE EMPEROR IN THE *UPRIGHT* POSITION WHICH DESCRIBES OUR 'VICTIM' JOHN

Turn to the description of The Emperor in the Greater Arcana (p. 52, Chapter 4) to remind yourself about this type of person. Incidentally, should this card appear for a female Questioner's description, don't be confused — the *traits* contained in this card will be applying to her at the time, thus indicating she has authority, ambition and power. Otherwise, the card represents a male influence — a man, when it appears in a spread.

CARD NO 2: INDICATING THE *DISTANT PAST* WAS THE *KING OF SWORDS* IN THE *UPRIGHT* POSITION

This describes John's background and past employment situation. Connections with law and communications, his position of authority in the Services where his skill directed others from his basis of original ideas, are all described by this card from the Lesser Arcana (p. 112). However, this card shows a possible problem — can you find it?

CARD NO 3: THE *IMMEDIATE PAST*, IS REPRESENTED BY THE *9 BATONS REVERSED*

This card highlights the frustrations John has encountered regarding employment after leaving the Services. The possible problem in the last card is emphasised here and should be noted. This is a typical example of how the Tarot shows the effect of the sequence from one card to the next.

CARD NO 4: PRESENT OBSTACLES AND INFLUENCES ARE SHOWN BY THE 7 BATONS UPRIGHT

Here we can see that John's attitude and ideas will be challenged severely by the interviewers so that it is necessary for him to research the nature of the job carefully to prepare himself for a testing time. If you read the meaning of this card on p. 103 you will see that any competition should be overcome providing he perseveres.

CARD NO 5: PRESENT OUTLOOK: 7 SWORDS IN THE UPRIGHT POSITION

This shows John what to expect at the interview and how he must prepare and strengthen himself in order to cope with close questioning, and again, this emphasises the previous card's message. This card shows progress but it needs courage and skill to communicate his abilities in a convincing manner.

CARD NO 6: FUTURE INFLUENCES ARE SHOWN BY THE HIGH PRIESTESS IN THE UPRIGHT POSITION

How fortunate for John that this card is in the *upright* position! Read the meaning and you will see why. Basically, it represents a woman's good influence which will enhance John's position at the interview. I asked him if this job could include the help or practical assistance of his wife and he thought that she would need to be a part of the position which was on offer. He also told me that their relationship supported mutual ideas and interests. I suggested that this area was of greater importance than he may have realised and that he and his wife should discuss her role at length so that he would be well prepared when interviewed.

CARD NO 7: THE FINAL RESULT SHOWN BY THE MAGICIAN IN THE UPRIGHT POSITION

We must remind ourselves at this point, of the question which was asked — 'What influences surround the interview?' The final result of these influences were shown by The Magician falling in the upright position which appears to be very favourable, showing positive developments leading to new beginnings and success.

We had enough information in this spread to encourage John to approach the interview with confidence providing he did his homework, especially regarding his wife's assets and qualifications. What happened? I heard nothing from him for some weeks until he telephone one weekend with interesting news.

The interview had been lengthy and had seemed to go well but they asked if they could meet his wife. This was accomplished, a further delay occurred and then he was recalled. Nail-biting stuff. The company explained that they were offering him a different post to the one advertised in his part of the country and would he consider moving further away for this better post where his wife would need to play a more important role? They accepted. We were all very delighted of course that the Tarot had finally come up trumps!

EXAMPLE 4: THE YEAR 2000 AD FOR THE UK

Looking ahead to the year 2000 AD will give you something really different to work out since we are dealing with the United Kingdom — a country, not a person, so the Astrol spread is ideal, looking at the general trends for the year, month by month. In Chapter 2, page 23, I suggested you might like to use this spread to look at our coming year, month by month with each card representing a particular department of life as well as a month.

In this case — *A Country* — the twelve cards (with a centre card for 'tone'), have to take on meanings which can deal with a country's concerns. The following list explains:

Card No 1: General conditions. Race character. Public health. Ordinary people.

Card No 2: National finances. Banks. Stock Exchange. Trade and commercial affairs. Financial fluctuations.

Card No 3: Communications: Postal, telecommunications, stocks and bonds, cars and traffic conditions, railway, newspapers, books. Countries which are 'neighbours'.

Card No 4: Agriculture, land use. Crops, weather, mines, disputes over land, public buildings. Opposition to Government. People opposing authority.

Card No 5: Educational facilities, theatres, sports centres, public morals, birth rate, speculation. Formal social functions. Ambassadors.

Card No 6: Public health. Civil Service, general working conditions. Armed services; strikes or disputes.

Card No 7: International relationships, negotiations and agreements, foreign trade. War. Marriages and divorces. Concerns of women generally.

Card No 8: Death rate, Suicides. Financial relations with foreign countries. Ceremonial functions for the dead.

Card No 9: Long-distance communications. National radio, television, cable satellite air and space traffic. Scientific institutions. Law and courts; trade and commerce, particularly long distance.

Card No 10: The Queen or head of the Royal Family. The Government. National celebrities. Aristocracy. National credit. Trade, power and diplomacy.

Card No 11: Parliament. House of Commons, legislation, local government, international friendships.

Card No 12: Prisons, crime, spies, reformatories. Hospitals, institutions. Secret negotiations, secret societies. Psychological state of the nation.

Using all of the 78 cards of the Tarot pack, I expressed the desire to see the year 2000 AD for the United Kingdom to be represented month by month. This is how the spread worked out:

CARD NO 1: THE CHARIOT (7) FOR JANUARY 2000

This card was in the upright position and tells us that general conditions in the country are beginning to improve, which means there must have been difficulties to overcome in the previous year (or years). Further effort and planning will be necessary.

CARD NO 2: THE WHEEL OF FORTUNE (10) REVERSED FOR FEBRUARY

This looks interesting: financial matters take a turn for the worse. Trade figures are not good. The Stock Exchange and banks are involved in unexpected events. Look at the opposite card, number 8, for financial relations with foreign countries and you see The Devil meaning we have (probably) a world-wide monetary problem.

CARD NO 3: THE KING OF SWORDS REVERSED FOR MARCH

This card represents a man who is skilled in communication but has a powerful, calculating manner with a strong intellectual authority. His connection is to do with the country's means of communication and he uses his power in an oppressive way. He could be pressing for some new legislation.

CARD NO 4: FIVE OF SWORDS FOR APRIL

Environmental difficulties: the general climate appears poor and the weather will affect spring sowing and crops. Structural damage to public buildings or a re-vamping, repairing and rebuilding is underway. Pressure from the Opposition party, also the general public, will not effect an immediate result over a current problem or dispute connected with events last month.

CARD NO 5: SEVEN OF CUPS FOR MAY

Little speculation is likely as choices are limited in making financial headway, although there is some room to manoeuvre, but only in a very restricted area. Circumstances surrounding the arts, cultural and recreational facilities suggest changes and there seems to be more of a national approach to these matters which hasn't yet been settled — or, the government's ideas for leisure are undergoing changes. A rather unsettled month in all sorts of ways.

CARD NO 6: SEVEN OF BATONS FOR JUNE

Competition will be high regarding employment and this card indicates perseverance. Any new businesses will have to be very well thought out and planned with faith in what is being attempted because risk factors are high. Taking chances will not come off. There could be disputes among workers. The army and navy appear to be restructured.

CARD NO 7: THE HANGED MAN (12) FOR JULY

A delay in international agreements where further negotiations are necessary, seems as if there is a state of uncertainty. The country appears to be working at a new role especially with regard to foreign trade.

CARD NO 8: THE DEVIL (5) FOR AUGUST

An undercurrent of problems regarding financial trade agreements requiring negotiation and re-examination with other countries. The death rate is high. There is some difficulty in obtaining co-operation from abroad.

CARD NO 9: TEMPERANCE (14) FOR SEPTEMBER

Negotiations are underway for trade and commerce connected with foreign countries. Space programmes, scientific knowledge and research in international co-operation show amazing new developments and understanding. Partnership agreements are likely to progress regarding the world communication systems.

CARD NO 10: JUSTICE (8) FOR OCTOBER

The government will be passing new legislation regarding recent trade agreements, matters connected with the Courts and revising the laws of the country. Justice will be seen to be done in many areas which are of public interest — this also involves well-known people. The status of the country improves. A woman is likely to be very important in bringing new strength and power in decision-making for the country's ultimate success.

CARD NO 11: THE FOOL FOR NOVEMBER

This card always means changes, and since this position represents Parliament, it could indicate a change of government — an election. In any case, new legislation which has an effect on local government affairs is highlighted. International agreement and the ability to form alliances still show challenges and unexpected developments. The intentions made by Parliament this month should bring progress and benefits to the country in the long-term. A new cycle begins.

CARD NO 12: JUDGEMENT (20) FOR DECEMBER

Any new laws concerning charitable institutions, hospitals and places of detention (prisons), should bring improvements. Alternative healing methods show acceptance and greater recognition under new laws. After a year when a great deal of undercover activity has been brought out into the open — this includes research, negotiations and realignment regarding the country's role in the world — the state of the nation shows achievement finishing the year on a much more hopeful note.

The *Centre* card giving an overall 'tone' for the year 2000 was the Sun (9). This implies success after overcoming difficulties which probably stem from earlier years — the late '90s.

You may like to set these cards out in a circle yourself and form your own opinions about them. Better still, spread your own layout for the UK in the year 2000 and compare notes. You are bound to get some different cards and they will match your psyche, intuition and your way of interpretation. Do work with Card No 1 through to Card No 12 and don't be tempted to interpret the cards at random, since, as you now know, there is an unfolding pattern. Write down each meaning or interpretation you make and keep the record for future reference.

If you find this circular spread aligned to Astrology too complicated, don't forget, you can invent your own methods and layouts — just remember to allow for a sequence to build up a picture, e.g. a card (or two) for the Distant Past, Immediate Past, Present Influences/ Obstacles and Future Influences, thus allowing the cards to help you and if you want a timing, be sure to state weeks, months or years as appropriate.

Always be quite clear in your mind what you wish the pattern to represent before you start — write everything down. That will help you take care of your logical, reasoning mind processes, thus allowing your intuitive mind to work later in giving you 'feelings' about the spread which you have dealt.

There are some amazing experts in the field of Tarot card readings, but don't be put off by anyone saying to you, 'I don't do the Tarot like that!'. It is your intent and the serious way in which you approach the art that counts.

THE DECISION-MAKING PROCESS

Making decisions about anything can sometimes be difficult, whether your concern is great or small. It all boils
down to how your 'decision-making' apparatus works.
Some people are more objective than others and some
are almost totally subjective. We might be very objective
about decisions in our working lives but when it comes
to personal matters involving emotions, we find ourselves and our personal burdens more difficult to handle.

In Chapter 1, I explained how the brain has basically
two halves where the left side deals with analytical and
verbal thought and the right deals with intuitive images,
symbols and patterns. Decision-making at work is based
on the availability of facts, but you still hear people say
they have a 'gut' feeling about something, despite the
indications of the facts. It is learning how to apply your
intuitive and 'knowing' nature *to* those facts which are
available which is the secret of decision-making success. By
consulting and practising with the Tarot yourself you will
develop and balance your feeling and analytical abilities.

If you consult an experienced Tarot card reader to
help your decision making — remember, you are not
only using their expertise — you are *pooling* your
intuitive resources and there should be serious, creative
and positive energy working, in which you are both
concerned. You are not letting an unusual-looking pack
of cards, nor an experienced reader take over your own
free will or decision-making — you are extending and
giving space to the matter which concerns you. The
cards act as the *focal point for your intuition* thus
allowing the matter in hand to clarify. You will have to
work at developing this sometimes rather dormant gift
to become 'clear seeing' (or clairvoyant), but it can be a
fascinating study as your progress.

Chapter 4

THE GREATER ARCANA
Pictures and Meanings

THE FOOL (Le Mat)
(sometimes called The Jester)

LE MAT.

MEANINGS

Upright:
There are imminent changes about to take place.
New beginnings: a new life-cycle concerning your
  destiny.
Unexpected developments. A challenge.
Decisions will have to be made.
A favourable* transformation of your circumstances.

* Note the cards which are placed on either side of the
Fool in your layout will give clues, e.g. if they are
fortunate cards, then decisions or change will bring
benefits and good progress can be made. Should the
cards either side be difficult ones, then careful consideration or planning is required in case you make a fool of
yourself!

Reversed:
Hesitate in proceeding further.
Neglect in responsibilities.
A faulty decision has been made.
Impulsive action leads to misfortune. Bad choice:
  problems.

The card as a person:
Someone who is creative, idealistic, has a good sense of
humour, a joker or comedian who is probably hiding
fear or insecurity. Young-at-heart. Rather irresponsible.

THE FOOL

This card has no number. The Fool represents both the
beginning and ending of the journey through life. Here
we have a carefree, inexperienced person who is open-
minded and innocent in the ways of the world, setting
off on his quest with his few possessions on his

shoulder. Some Tarot packs show this card as a Joker or Jester, which again, conveys an irresponsible, pleasure-seeking attitude.

The Fool's journey into the unknown shows inexperience setting off to gain experience and self-expression. He is free to choose between good and evil, wisdom and foolishness, so that when this card appears in a spread it denotes change through choice and can have an effect of altering or colouring the cards on each side of its position.

When the journey has ended, the symbolism of The Fool can be viewed as a transformation. He is now totally aware and in harmony with himself and the universe knowing he has achieved immortality, so he is once again carefree and innocent of the drabness of the world, for he sees only perfection.

MEANINGS

Upright:

Expect developments.

You can adapt, arrange or plan matters with confidence.

The necessary willpower is available to start and follow through something with confidence, leading to success.

New beginnings requiring tenacity which will develop your personality.

Reversed:

Beware of using your skills unwisely and for the wrong reasons.

Be realistic: insufficient willpower to succeed.
Opportunities are limited through lack of skill and weak
   will, so that delays and disappointments are inevitable.

The card as a person:
A dual character. Appears to be self-confident. Has
individuality and creativity with willpower to act in a
positive manner. Likes to entertain others. A 'loner'.
Inwardly, has original ideas, keeps his cards 'close to his
chest' and explores new ways of doing things by
manipulating or manoeuvring, for he wishes to improve
and transform everything that interests him.

THE MAGICIAN

The Magician represents the first phase of experience in
life where the task is to learn how to live in the
environment and be responsible for all action which is
taken. Through the use of the intellect (the mind), and
development of the physical body (the senses), there is
a choice of balancing the two, and here, over-develop-
ment of the ego can take place.

   There is a duality here — outwardly, the seeker on
the path in search of wisdom, or inwardly, a seeker in
search of power who manipulates people and circumstances for his or her own ends.

   The symbolism of the picture endeavours to show
what we have at our disposal to equip us for our
journey through life: The man, standing behind a table
upon which are placed the 'tools of his trade', which
represent his mental, physical, emotional and creative
attributes in the form of a Baton, a Coin, a Sword and a
Cup — the four suits of the Lesser Arcana section of the
Tarot pack — which are also symbolic of the elements:
Fire, Earth, Air and Water.

MEANINGS

Upright:

Hidden factors are in operation which are full of hope
bringing strength to the matter in hand.

Understanding brought about by information coming to
you from your intuition or through inspiration, which
will solve problems in an unexpected way.

Common sense is operating.

A woman who is wise — perhaps a friend or a
counsellor — can assist you or influence you.

Reversed:
A reluctance to seek advice. Selfishness.
The emotions are in a state of imbalance and difficulty.
You are being rather short-sighted regarding personal
problems: an emotional block.
A state of being unaware of your true feelings.
The influence of a woman who uses emotional
blackmail.

The card as a person:
A wise, creative woman who is not only caring but upon
whom you can rely to give you the right answers. A
valued woman friend. A mature woman of common
sense, who gives guidance, inspiration and counsel.

THE HIGH PRIESTESS

The High Priestess represents the perfect woman,
source of all wisdom and knowledge which is gained
through imagination, intuition and inspiration. This
comes from the unconscious mind through dreams and
visions to the conscious reasoning mind as enlightenment. So the search for self-awareness, if it is to be
pursued in the right way, must come from within the
self, where wisdom and knowledge — the understanding of the laws of cause and effect and the true order of
the Universe — is gradually revealed.

The High Priestess is often depicted in the picture
holding a book — the Book of Wisdom. She is the
feminine principle following on from the Magician
(Card No 1), who represents the masculine principle,
and who, you will remember, is seeking wisdom.

The challenge shown by this card is to seek the other
half of oneself, to understand both the male and female
forces within ourselves so that by bringing these
together through search and challenge in human

existence, we can thereby gain wisdom. The picture on the card shows a woman dressed in robes with a type of crown on her head.

MEANINGS

Upright:

The matter in hand will be fruitful. Progress is made so that accomplishment is achieved. Marriage. Motherhood, or a sense of well-being.

Your domestic situation is stable and secure.

Further progress can be made based on the structures in your life that are already established.

Reversed:

Upheavals on the domestic front. Domination by a woman.

Financial difficulties.

Delays in your progress with the matter in hand, due to

indecision or lack of concentration.
A need to face up to reality.

The card as a person:
A woman of stable character with a motherly, caring manner. She is creative, a homemaker and knows the values which are important in life. She considers the feelings of others, is sympathetic and dedicated to her family's comfort and well-being, and in a wider context is concerned about the welfare of society as a whole.

THE EMPRESS

The Empress represents the Great Mother, guardian of birth and motherhood. This challenge in the search for wisdom in human existence is where the process of discrimination really begins to develop.

The test is to be able to realise that our material world is really a reflection of Heaven: 'as above, so below' and that we *can* make heaven on earth. It is achieved by being positively creative, by caring and nurturing with both people and the environment which supports us. By observing the order of Nature, respecting the cycles of the seasons and by realising there is a right time for everything in life to occur.

The essence of Love and recognition of the true values which should be placed upon everything is embodied in this process. It is the ability to *feel* the reason for life as well as intellectualise about it.

Life is everywhere, mind is everywhere — feel it!

The negative aspect of this card's symbolism is to fail to see or understand the need to express oneself in a creative way or care about anything outside ourselves.

THE EMPEROR: 4 (IIII)

MEANINGS

Upright:

Power can be acquired through your past experience and knowledge or 'know-how'.

Self-control can be applied over the emotions in order to achieve your goals and ambitions.

Strength and willpower are available.

Assistance or advice from someone in a position of authority will help your present situation.

Reversed:

No impression can be made at this time. Your position is weak.

Ineffective and unrealistic.

Take care with your emotional reactions.
Don't waste time and energy on unproductive things.

The card as a person:
A powerful, authoritative man who has put a lot of
energy into creating and maintaining his world. A good
organiser and leader involved in planning for others. He
is sensitive to others' feelings and abilities; he bases his
decisions on facts, is logical and is seen to be effective
and is respected for his 'man management'. A father
figure — a man of influence.

THE EMPEROR

The Emperor represents creation through reason, logic
and the will as opposed to The Empress whose creativity
is through love and feelings. They complement each
other. This is the masculine principle again, the father-
figure. Power is the name of the game and this
challenge in life is to understand how to wield it in the
right way. Facts, figures, strength and discipline build up
his position in the outside world and his influence upon
other people. He is reliable, except in circumstances
where emotions and feelings abound. He represents the
masculine world.

A woman needs to be aware of the challenge of the
father-figure in her life and rather than be dominated by
it, she should develop will and courage herself to
complement her feminine attributes. The aim for both
sexes is ultimately to achieve a balance between the two
types of force: masculine and feminine. At this point it
may be helpful to be reminded of what was said in
Chapter 1, that the brain has two hemispheres which see
the world in different ways; the left side specialises in
verbal and analytical thought, while the right side
specialises in the understanding of patterns and intuition.
The left side analyses over time and space and codes

memory in linguistic description, while the right codes memory in images.

A well-balanced person operates either parts of the brain according to the task in hand, or uses them in conjunction with one another. I feel that this is also an example of combining the masculine and feminine principles and symbolises the Empress and the Emperor.

The card shows the crowned Emperor seated upon a throne out in the open air. In his hand a sceptre and beside him, a shield. The sceptre is the symbol of his masculinity, and the shield is a sign of his authority. He wears badges of office and the sword of power at his side showing the importance of his place in the world.

MEANINGS

Upright:

You are supported by wisdom and can be enlightened
   regarding the present circumstances.

Something will be revealed which will serve to expand
   and improve the situation.

Inspiration — a revelation.

A mature man of a 'spiritual' nature, who is kind,
   compassionate or generous can help you.

Reversed:
The truth has been distorted and misrepresented.
Bad advice has been, or will be, given.
You are vulnerable, perhaps unconventional, regarding the matter.
Don't overextend yourself.

The card as a person:
A counsellor, teacher or an advisor of mature years; sometimes connected with the Law. Someone upon whom you can rely for sound advice. A practical person of sound morals who bases his understanding on tradition with a wide knowledge of the physical, emotional and mental make-up of a man. A man who is particular, and lives an orderly and well-planned way.

JUPITER

Jupiter, sometimes called the High Priest, is complementary to the High Priestess and this 5th challenge is aimed at the abilities of maturity, where all that has been learned through past experience has brought wisdom.

What matters now, is how that wisdom is applied. As we move from one stage to another, our intent and motives are increasingly tested by people and circumstances. This develops our sense of discrimination yet again — there are always choices to be made. For example, there is an awareness of our own moral code — this may not be the same as other people's, but we may think it right for everyone. The danger here is to force or insist upon our way of thinking. We should rather not judge another, but be discriminating with advice if asked, and allow others their point of view. Despite wisdom and maturity, a superior attitude should be avoided.

Nevertheless, the values of this stage are rewarding. Inspiration and encouragement can be given to others through teaching, informing and listening. The capacity for deep thought, contemplation and a certain spirituality has developed so that new ideas and inspiration flow in to solve one's own or others' problems.

The card shows a mature man who is seated and adopting a 'thinking' pose with his hand resting on his bearded chin. He wears a type of crown showing he is a person of some authority and at his feet is a sacred eagle. His beard and the eagle both signify wisdom.

THE LOVERS: 6 (VI)

MEANINGS

Upright:

Choices must be made with care. There is a battle between reason and intuition and you must respect your feelings and intuition this time.

A flash of inspiration solves a problem.

There is possible temptation, predicament or even yearning.

If in doubt, remember — love conquers all!

A meeting leading to a possible romance.

Reversed:

Separation. You can't have the best of both worlds.

Failure to see a way out of a difficulty in a close

relationship. Severe temptation makes choosing diffi-
cult.
Your present plans are unwise.
Don't evade the issue.

The card as people:
This is a 'situation' card: a young man and young woman
who care for each other, but there is a problem. There
is a third party which can be an older man or woman, or
it can be something else like a problem coming
between them. This brings a dilemma with a hesitation
about going forward because of the past, or a reluctance
to make a decision because a problem is interfering
with their progress.

THE LOVERS

The Lovers symbolise the dilemma of choice. Their past
— their childhood — beckons, but Cupid overhead
guards their love. The security and comfort of what is
known, where decisions have previously been made for
them, casts doubts about going forward with faith in
their idea of love. It is a challenge of faith in the self and
allowing love (which is both a creative and compassionate energy) to carry them forward with dedication and
purpose. In order to win through, a sacrifice has to be
made, that of being able to leave the past behind them.
If this challenge is too great, then it isn't the right time
to proceed and the duo will move apart.
   The same, or similar, situations will repeat themselves
until faith in the power of love, which overcomes all
things, is understood. Any prolonged delay in the
decision will attract a pressure of circumstances and
events which will force the issue anyway. Some thought
is required to grasp this 6th challenge upon life's
journey. The loving experience in all its forms comes to

everyone in different ways. If enough love is applied to any difficult situation, then the way forward opens up.

The picture on this card shows a young man and woman holding hands. Behind them is a figure, arm upraised as if calling them back. They pause at a crossroads and appear to be looking back. Above them is a guardian angel — Cupid, representing Love.

MEANINGS

Upright:

You have already overcome a challenge or difficulty.

Success through your own efforts and hard work in the
past.

The goal is in sight — watch your timing and continue
to work and plan carefully, then success will follow.

The worst is over but you cannot rest in the present
position without further effort.

Reversed:

You will be unsuccessful.

Unexpected difficulties halt your progress towards
success.

You have tried to force issues or force your ideas upon others.

There has been inattention to detail and you have overlooked the points of view of others.

The card as a person:
One who has control over the personality and emotions so there is harmony between the mental and physical bodies. A person with a practical understanding in the laws of society who knows how to benefit from them. A person of substance/material success who knows what they want. Reversed, this card describes an oppressor who uses position and power against anyone who opposes or challenges them.

THE CHARIOT

The number 7 assigned to this card is the number of the universe which signifies a total, a completeness. The dilemma placed by card number 6, now shows the ability to make the right choice and to go forward as a more mature individual. This stage represents a condition where there is harmony between the body (the physical) and the soul (spiritual) parts of an individual. Through endeavour and then experience, the person has trained both the intellect and instincts to operate in harmony. There is self-discipline of mind and body which gives self-confidence and self-reliance when facing problems and coming through them successfully.

Having achieved success in many areas, the pitfalls can now show up as the power to manipulate others, to make others 'dance to your tune' and to use self-reliance and the development of personal power to oppress others or force them to act for your own advantage. This will naturally restrict the development of personality and over-develop the ego. The lesson here is to remain aware of the need for humility.

MEANINGS

Upright:

Use your judgement and sense of fairness with the ability to remain neutral when exercising your negotiating powers to get a just outcome.

The truth of the matter will be revealed.

Justice will be seen to be done.

A matter of law which will be successful.

Agreements or legal matters should proceed.

Reversed:

There will be legal difficulties involving some delay in progress.

Problems with administration regarding your present circumstances.
False information; lack of attention to the law.
There is a lack of perspective.

The card as a person:
Someone who is known for their sense of justice and fair play. An adjudicator. A negotiator who has integrity and sound moral judgement. Someone who upholds the law. A magistrate. Someone who is reasonable, well-balanced and who remains true to their convictions.

JUSTICE

This 8th stage depicted by the figure of Justice represents the balance and completion of maturity. Although this is a fulfillment of all that has been worked for, by the achievement of the goals set in earlier years, there is something still missing. When a person has worked for and made a secure place in the world and reaches middle age, there is a looking back. Why? Their needs and ambitions have been met in a conscious way in the material world, but now the soul, the unconscious, tries to surface, and this is the challenge for the second half of life — finding the inner person.

The total balance of a person concerns the law of destiny and of the universe. The Sword of Justice is two-edged — it cuts both ways — and the time has come to develop the inner, or spiritual, part. Eventually when the person comes 'to be weighed in the balance', the wholeness of the physical and spiritual bodies is the true total of achievement where the scales will truly balance the whole person. This leads to the next stage of the quest symbolised by card number 9, the Hermit.

MEANINGS

Upright:
Withdrawal. Delay.
Do not proceed unless all has been carefully thought through and planned.
A wise person can give you counsel, understanding and strength.
Play your cards 'close to your chest'. Be discreet.
The time is not right to forge ahead.
Take stock, pause and plan at this time and listen to your conscience.

Reversed:

Impatience.

Inadequate planning.

Impulsive action taken without considering the consequences.

The way is blocked at the moment for further progress.

A more mature attitude is required — common sense is lacking.

Sound help and advice has been overlooked or refused.

The card as a person:

A wise man, counsellor, teacher or a spiritual person who can answer your questions and throw some light upon spiritual matters. For example, your priest, a man connected with religions, beliefs or philosophical subjects. A guru. One who understands the many facets and pitfalls of life.

THE HERMIT

The Hermit as card number 9 symbolises the final stage of the first half of the journey through life, 9 being the last of the single numbers. The outward journey that started with the Fool, reached a turning point at card number 8 when the Scales of Justice indicated favourably that the time had come to proceed with the second phase of the quest — the inward journey.

For the first time, the dark night of the soul is encountered, where only faith can support the loneliness The Hermit represents. By isolation, meditation and giving the self some space from the outer world and its comforts, can the imagination, intuition and inspiration fully flourish. Inner vision and wisdom develop naturally as the person moves towards the centre of his or her being — the soul. The challenge here is to remain aware and open-minded, allowing enlightenment to flow in. There is often a crisis of will at this point where it is necessary to let go of some previously held, fixed ideas and concepts which block progress. Becoming 'enlightened' is to receive inspirational answers to questions which have plagued a person. Now he listens to the inner voice.

The picture shows a bearded, mature man dressed in a simple habit, holding a lantern in his right hand. The way is dark, the path is stony and he holds a staff in his other hand to guide him. It is interesting to compare this figure with that of The Fool who represented the beginning of the journey into the outer world with his childlike qualities. Now, the beginning of the inner journey commences with only the light of intuition (the lantern), and the staff, symbolising inner wisdom, to guide him. He is sometimes called the Guardian of Time. He has freed himself from the past and he is learning to live in the present.

MEANINGS

Upright:

Destiny carries you forward into a new cycle, a new
    beginning.

Whatever will be, will be.

Unexpected events could occur about which you can do
    nothing but which can have a fortunate effect upon
    your progress.

Lucky chance. A problem solved.

Reversed:
Failure.
A turn for the worse.
Unexpected and unfortunate events.
Bad luck.
Things won't turn out as you expect.
A sequence of events must now occur before progress
   can be made.

To recognise the card personally:
This is a 'situation' card, where just when you thought
things should get better, unexpected events and circumstances arise which plunge you right back where you
started. Eventually, what appears to be a stroke of good
fortune saves the situation and lifts you into the start of
something new — a new beginning. This is the cycle of
destiny.

THE WHEEL OF FORTUNE

The wheel or circle is the symbol of perfection. This
card, number 10, signifies both a new beginning and an
ending, or, completion of the previous cards. (Note that
the Wheel of Fortune has 8 spokes representing the 8
previous stages with the hub of the wheel as the 9th).
The second half of the journey begins with this card and
it shows the law of cause and effect, it depicts the order
and continuous flow or motion of both human life and
of the universe, and in fact says that we have an ongoing
situation.

The Wheel of Fortune in human existence symbolises
birth and death, the beginning and ending, but what
about the middle? We know that birth must ultimately
end in death and the portion in between is uncertain.
Once we are on the wheel of life, we are always striving
and hoping that something better will turn up — some
good fortune perhaps. We cling to forms of security

which make life feel more certain — we think we know where we're going until something unexpected happens to change our expectations.

Ultimately, when we have experienced many types of birth and death, we realise, hopefully, that *nothing* is certain. The only thing that is certain, is uncertainty. By accepting this, life becomes more free — and living in the present, in the 'now', widens the quality of each moment and its value is appreciated giving a more harmonious existence. However, this is not the final goal. The Hermit was searching for illumination from his visions and dreams and the Wheel of Fortune illustrates them. Through his self-examination, his inward visions are brought out into the conscious mind and his questions are answered about the law and structure of human existence and of the universe.

FORTITUDE: 11 (XI)
(Strength, La Force)

MEANINGS

Upright:

Have courage and strength in the present situation.

Someone challenges your present position — hidden
forces could be at work.

Remain steadfast and true to yourself.

A risk could be involved if you are to succeed, so quiet
determination is indicated.

Inner purpose could be assailed by doubts and fears,
but remain resolute.

Reversed:
Loss of opportunity.
Lack of faith.
Weakness and lack of courage to face the present situation.
Hidden temptations will lead to failure.

The card as a person:
A self-disciplined, courageous individual who can be unemotional yet compassionate when dealing with circumstances or people. Reliable and discerning. A person who is kind, has a 'heart of gold' and serves others willingly at the right time, or when required. Someone who has the ability to act as a conciliator or negotiator. Strength without violence.

FORTITUDE

This challenge, symbolised by Fortitude, is having courage in the face of danger — the mental power of endurance. It is having the ability to be objective, to see both sides of the coin when faced with a challenge from a person or a circumstance, or even dealing with one's own inner problems which have been deeply buried in the subconscious. The power that is used to deal with any of these examples, is the all-conquering power of love. It is learning to love oneself first and being able to apply compassion to any person situation or circumstance when challenged — even unjustly.

The previous card, the Wheel of Fortune emphasised the ability to face uncertainty, and the Hermit's self-examination through his inward journey emphasised having to face the dark or shadowy side of man's nature by questioning and becoming enlightened. So it is through detachement and self-examination that self-realisation comes (The Hermit), and the confrontation of unseen forces and uncertainty (The Wheel of

Fortune), that sets Fortitude as the challenge at this stage. Fortitude is the second of the Virtues to appear in the Greater Arcana, Justice, Temperance and Prudence being the other three.

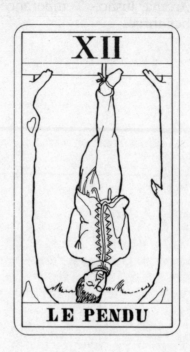

MEANINGS

Upright:

You can readjust your present position to suit changing
  circumstances — there is flexibility.

A delay or suspension of activity is taking place.

Listen to your intuition for guidance at this time.

There is uncertainty and a need to see others' points of
  view, or see yourself in a new light.

Take your time to readjust your position.

Reversed:

Failure to give up something: selfishness.

Material matters have caught up with you.
Lack of effort.
Your understanding is faulty.

The card as a person:
Someone who seems to live in another world — a dreamer. A person who you cannot seem to get to know, yet should you seek their advice you realise they have great experience of life, wisdom and truth. They have the ability to point out another way of looking at things and give you another point of view.

THE HANGED MAN

This is a strange symbol denoting renewal which is brought about by the act of suspension or delaying further action for the time. The man has chosen to rest somewhere between Heaven and Earth safely suspended by one foot from a tree (the Tree of Life). In this position he has no contact with the earth (his past understanding or consciousness), and being upside-down denotes the reversal of all his previously held beliefs and values. This requires courage and faith and signifies the death of the old self — a turning point, so that a transformation can take place. (Think of a chrysalis at rest before the beautiful butterfly breaks out in all its glory). This is a difficult stage to cope with in the outside world because you can be seen to be 'different' in your ideas and understanding of life. There is abandonment to your spiritual convictions and you rest in total faith. A sacrifice has been made, but entered into willingly showing total freedom from desire.

The picture shows the man suspended upside-down from one foot which is tied by a rope to a tree. His hands are behind his back — perhaps secured, but his face shows calm resignation and a halo surrounds his head on some cards, denoting his faith.

DEATH: 13 (XIII)
(La Mort. Transformation)

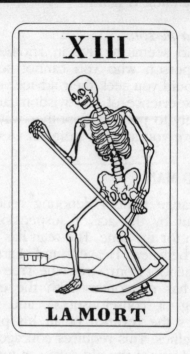

MEANINGS

Upright:

An ending, in order to make way for a new beginning.
Unexpected changes clear the way for progress.
Conditions around you will be transformed.
A new era begins.
Possible loss of material/financial resources.

Reversed:

Fate seems to take over your affairs.
Something or someone is removed because you failed
   to clear up or clarify a difficult matter.

Faulty planning results in a downfall of fortune.
Recovery from illness or catastrophe.

Further help on how to read this card:
Very seldom does this card actually denote the death of
a person, unless your question is aimed at such an
answer. Many people view this card with some concern
when it comes up in a reading. It should be viewed as a
necessary change from an old, outworn condition to
make way for something new. It is a very positive card
showing the underlying continuance of all things,
representing the point at which the cycle changes (as for
example in the seasons). This card is so often a blessing
in disguise.

DEATH

This symbol tends to make people uncomfortable when
it appears in a layout of Tarot cards, but we should
remind ourselves about the previous card, the Hanged
Man which leads us to this stage. His attitude was to be
able to see things in the opposite way, helping us to
realise that a) things are not always what they seem, and
b) try taking the opposite viewpoint to understand what
is happening. The opposite to Death is Birth. There
must be an ending before there is a beginning, or, in
the transformation of one thing to another, there is a
maturing energy at work where the old, outworn is
discarded and the new is developed. It is set out in
Nature, year after year, with the cycle of the seasons. The
Wheel of Fortune describes the 'ongoing situation'
where experiences teach us to observe this inevitability.
The future is set by the seeds of the present and the
present springs from the past showing a continuance of
life. Life is therefore full of opportunity.

Many people also dislike the number 13 which is
given to this card, thinking it to be unfortunate. Others

think it lucky for them, so let's have a look at this number. It is made up of 1 and 3, when added, makes 4. Numbers are used in many ancient traditions to describe a quality and quantity, or as a basic principle from which the world proceeds. In particular, a mathematician or physicist understands their world from that viewpoint. The number 4 is defined as a total, a completion, perfection and the number of earth, among other things. Numbers are the primary substance of the universe. So you can see, by looking at things in a positive way, rather than a negative way, our viewpoint can be expanded and changed by further information, symbolism and research.

MEANINGS

Upright:

Negotiation and discussion are necessary to make further progress.

A helpful sharing of thoughts, feelings and ideas.

A possible partnership.

Some moderation in actions is required at this point: a balancing and blending is necessary before proceeding towards your goal.

Take everything into account before disclosing your interest.

Reversed:

Conflicting attitudes can arise in both personal and occupational affairs.

Inability to handle the present situation, or other people.

Disharmony surrounds the present circumstances.

Beware impatience or prejudice.

The card as a person:

A person who is an expert in his or her chosen field, having great knowledge in all areas of life as well as being both practical and in tune with all social conditions in the community. Someone you might think of as your 'guardian angel' for a time.

TEMPERANCE

The old meaning of the word temperance comes from the verb 'to temper' — to mix in the right proportions, to blend or to modify by blending and mixing. This is how the card should be viewed, for the symbolism of the picture is conveying this blending and mixing of the waters of new life from one container (the unconscious) to another (the conscious). This action follows on from card number 13 – Death, where there was an ending resulting in a new seed of life, and now the continuance and the renewal are taking place. The figure on the card can be viewed as the Angel of Time, blending the past, present and future as total existence. The waterfall in the picture emphasises the flow of the past through the present into the future.

MEANINGS

Upright:

There is something or someone working against your interests of which you may be unaware.

Your present plans are based on the wrong reasons or intent.

Your inner feelings, or fears of insecurity, are colouring the matter and further progress is blocked.

A situation which can end in disaster unless you re-examine your role and attitude.

Reversed:

You can overcome present difficulties.

Realisation and enlightenment are at hand, which shows hope for further progress.

Your present fears are unnecessary and unfounded.

The card as a person:

A difficult, moody person: one who acts through the destructive emotions of anger, fear, hate, jealousy, worry, envy, lust and even grief. Someone who is known as a 'stirrer'. A person who projects his or her problems onto someone else, who makes you feel oppressed and who is adept at controlling others against their will.

THE DEVIL

The symbolism of this card is sometimes frightening because it describes the power of hidden instincts, hidden emotions, or hidden desires. This is the energy within ourselves which can attack in moments of crisis. Negativity can flood in and all the ground gained before, in terms of seeking wisdom and knowledge, is held back at that moment.

This can represent a serious crossroads, where one can use all the power that has been worked for and gained, and redirect it in the wrong way — for selfish, material or moral purposes. The secret is, that all forces which are ranged against you, either from outside or from within you, cannot withstand the power of pure love.

Emmett Fox wrote *'There is no difficulty that enough love will not conquer ... if only you could love enough you would be the happiest and most powerful being in the world'*. The power of positive thinking is part of this secret which is to transmute — to change to another form and allow love and light to change dark thoughts, depressions or primitive instincts into powers of a new kind which give and bring new life. Lucifer is the opposing side of the Devil and the bringer of Light. This card shows that the dangers are not over yet and that we must look at the forces of nature within ourselves, cultivate them, not let them run wild and above all, respect them. They should not enslave us. Have courage. The next card, The Tower will help unfold more meaning relevant to this one.

MEANINGS

Upright:

An unexpected and sudden event which reveals misplaced trust, or destroys previously held ideas or beliefs.

Some breakdown occurring around you which will make way for something new.

Loss of security and stability — possibly financial.

Influences around you are destructive or negative.

A setback in your circumstances.

Reversed:
You are trapped in a difficult situation.
At present there seems to be no way out.
Need to adapt to the present situation.

The card as a situation:
This describes a happening, event or circumstance which appears to be beyond control. The forces of nature are usually involved, either outward and visible like a storm, or inward, inside you, where you feel shocked or bereft due to some prevailing circumstance. In a reading, you must note the cards either side of the Tower which will give you clues as to how this will give its effect.

THE TOWER

This card symbolises power and is an extension of the previous card, The Devil, in that it describes the act of enlightenment (Lucifer bringing light) or lightning striking as in the picture. It flashes suddenly, striking the Tower and destroying it. The Tower represents all that has been built up during the quest for the meaning of life through all the trials. Contact is made. The flash of truth strikes at our very core and in that second we may understand, but, if the lightning blinded us because the power was too intense, then a great deal is lost since our understanding and preparation wasn't good enough to withstand the unexpected.

Let us look at it in a similar way with reference to our environment — the outward and visible. We can see the forces of nature at work with every passing moment. The elements of Fire, Earth, Air and Water make up the constituents of nature on our planet. We harness them all in a variety of ways. Once we cease to respect them on any level, they work against us. For example, on the very simple level of 'playing with fire', think what can happen with an ordinary box of matches! The element of Fire is wrapped up in the meaning of this card: the Fire of Life — contact is made with the meaning of life, the centre of our search. An initiation by fire. Is it too hot to handle?

MEANINGS

Upright:

The future looks bright bringing fulfillment to your hopes and wishes.

Inspiration and insight will be given either directly to you, or from a friend whom you can trust.

Your scope is increased, your horizons widen towards good fortune in the future according to the present situation.

Reversed:

Your ambitions and hopes remain unfulfilled.

An inability to progress due to fixed ideas and a mind closed to opportunities.

A need to accept that the present situation is not conducive to progress.

The card as a person:
Someone who has the ability to 'heal' others physically, mentally and spiritually. A person who is far-sighted, clear-sighted (clairvoyant), and who conveys hope and inspiration to others through their work, or as a friend.

THE STAR

The symbolism of the pouring of the Water of Life into a lake is one of healing after the initiation by Fire as represented in the previous card, The Tower. Now the waters of baptism signify the journey is nearing completion — faith has been tested and the stars of hope shine down.

All the symbols on this card show that there is understanding on all levels — physically, mentally and spiritually, and the mind is open and able to receive new ideas and new concepts as well as bring inspiration and encouragement to others. To reach this level of understanding is to be like a star shining down, radiating light and wisdom to others. The Star represents hope, faith, love and optimism in the future. Wherever it appears in a layout of cards in an upright position, good fortune prevails.

THE MOON: 18 (XVIII)

MEANINGS

Upright:
Your faith in yourself is challenged by the present
  circumstances.
Act upon your intuition at this time, it is more reliable.
There is insincerity and possible deception about.
Unforeseen setbacks.
Hidden danger or hidden enemies are involved.

Reversed:
Inability to progress through lack of faith in yourself and
  your abilities.
Silly mistakes have been made.

Deception is recognised for what it is.
You have taken advantage of someone.

The card as a situation:

This card represents a point at which there is a calm before something decisive will happen. A time of reflection. Being realistic about the past and not wishing for what might have been. A turning point of great importance in life where feelings and intuition are uppermost in carrying you forward with faith and conviction in yourself despite other people's doubts or desires. The Moon can also reflect how you feel emotionally about a current situation — perhaps being swayed and held back because of them. The question 'Do you know how you really *feel* about this?' could be asked of your client according to the type of reading required.

THE MOON

This card shows a peaceful scene and symbolically represents the place where we find ourselves when between life and death. This is another turning point in life where all past memories come up for review, so The Moon can often refer to a life-and-death situation within the current existence, which has to be dealt with and clarified. In a way, we could find ourselves in a sort of limbo and you could find that something must be reviewed, understood and accepted for what it is — letting go of the past with memories and emotions in order to allow this moment of limbo to lead you into the future.

This part of the journey through life is not fully illuminated because the path is lit only by the Moon. It leads the traveller toward two towers (or in some cards, a building with a doorway is illustrated). The crayfish, often shown entering a pool of water depicts our spirit entering into the Pool of Memory to review all that has taken place in our life in the past, so before we can proceed, this reply has to take place. Between the towers or the pillars of the doorway is the threshold which has guardians (shown by two dogs) who challenge anyone wishing to proceed. They will not attack but try to put you off. You must have enough conviction and inner purpose to go towards something better.

This path is the way of the true self, that part of us which is eternal when one can know, accept and be able to say, 'This is truly me and I am going home'. The challenge that this card represents is to be steadfast and true to yourself despite setbacks, illusions and deceptive influences around you.

L

MEANINGS

Upright:
Accomplishment and achievement regarding the matter in hand.
Success after overcoming obstacles or difficulties.
The outcome will give you satisfaction and pleasure.
Your imagination and innovation brings rewards.
Safe arrival.

Reversed:
Failure due to some misjudgement regarding the matter.
Unhappiness for the time being.
Cancelled plans.
Don't kid yourself — real success still eludes you.

The card as a situation:

The attainment of some goal or objective is recognised and a successful conclusion has been reached. There is a feeling of power, well-being and even glory, but this transformation has to be maintained. The reward cannot be taken away because it has been rightly and justly earned, but the very peak of success does change everything around you and within you, so even now, the quality of attainment has to be judged on its own merits, giving the ability to cope with and maintain this transformation.

THE SUN

At last, the traveller reaches the Sun to become a source of light to others, whereas he was only able to reflect that light when at the previous stage — the Moon. The Sun and Moon symbolise positive and negative, male and female principles which are now united to become one. This means the traveller has become united within himself and has reached full development. The Chinese Yin Yang symbol aptly demonstrates these two principles resting in harmony and complete as a whole.

Each person in human existence carries the male and female poles — positive and negative qualities in the physical body. Man is also made up of a spiritual body, a mental body and an emotional body as described by the elements and the suits of the Lesser Arcana:

Physical Body: Earth (Coins)
Spiritual Body: Fire (Batons)
Mental Body: Air (Swords)
Emotional Body: Water (Cups)

On the spiritual journey, through the trials and experience of life and the wisdom and knowledge gained, the seeker gains the unification of the two opposite poles or principles (male and female or positive and negative), and at the same time has balanced and united all of the parts of which he is made. In so doing, he has become one, or a 'whole', thus gaining immortality.

Looking at the number assigned to this card — 19, if you add 1 to 9 it equals 10 which in turn reduces to 1 — the one or 'whole'.

MEANINGS

Upright:
Achievement and improvement to the present conditions.
Your present concerns show development bringing new
  conditions, hope and happiness.
A rebirth of either yourself, your plans, or projects
  according to the circumstances.
A legal matter is favourable.
You have to account for your success or achievement.

Reversed:
Delay or postponement of the matter in hand.
Face the facts — wasted opportunities in the past cannot
  produce the required results.

Indecision regarding the present circumstances.
The outcome of a legal matter is unfavourable.
Something is taken from you.

The card as a situation:
Quite simply, this can imply a court of law where
someone or something is being judged. In another way,
the card symbolises an attainment which is judged solely
on its merits. One has always to be accountable for
everything — the law of cause and effect operates all the
time. However, the angel on the card symbolises
protection (a guardian angel), who is bringing good
news by blowing upon the trumpet, if the card is in the
upright position.

JUDGEMENT

Having reached the final goal — the Sun, where all that
has been learned and experienced is integrated, this
stage of Judgement refers to the continuing impulse of
being creative even though achievement has been
attained.

Like the angel which hovers over the scene on the
card, from space, we have the ability to see our position
clearly, as if we had climbed a mountain and were
looking at the view spread out below and all around. We
have achieved the detachment of wisdom to see every
condition in ourselves and the environment. We have
gained inner peace because we have become our own
conscience and at one with everything that is. The
experience of the emotions and desires has led to the
realisation that inner happiness is of the spiritual part of
the body which had gradually developed through
radiating love and warmth (the Sun), to all living
creatures and the environment.

Both the outer journey of everyday existence and
experiences, and the inner journey of listening to the

'inner voice' — developing the intuitive, spiritual nature, brings the rebirth or transformation. This means freedom and happiness in a unity of the soul — the part of you that is *really* you, which has found its home at last.

THE WORLD 21 (XXI)

MEANINGS

Upright:

You have reached the final goal and finished the course successfully.

You receive recognition and acclaim for your efforts.

The successful ending of a cycle of circumstances and events.

Your hopes and dreams come true.

Reversed:

There is a lack of foresight and planning regarding the present circumstances.

Your endeavours have reached a fixed point and cannot continue.

Failure in achieving what you set out to do.

The card as a situation:
You are the centre of attention because of finally attaining something for which you have worked hard and long. Honour and admiration are awarded to you because of your success. This card can also represent an event which brings a cycle of destiny to an end and which fulfills all expectations.

THE WORLD

This card represents one's hopes and wishes eventually coming true. The quest is completed. When this card appears in a spread it is very fortunate, no matter how simple the question. In the picture the central figure, surrounded by a circle of flowers, implies by symbolism the attainment of having become one with all that is: the Cosmos, the Universe. The bull, the lion, the eagle and the man each occupy a corner of the card not only representing the four corners of the Earth, but also the signs of the Zodiac: Taurus, Scorpio, Aquarius and Leo whose elements are Earth, Water, Air and Fire. In Astrology these are known as the Fixed signs which are the Powers of the Zodiac, Lords of the corners of creation and their virtues are force and tenacity.

As previously stated the four elements are assigned to the four suits in the Lesser Arcana — Batons (Fire), Coins (Earth), Swords (Air), and Cups (Water), denoting the exercise of the will, the desire for material comfort and security, the exercise of the mental processes and the emotions and feelings.

To sum up the symbolism of this card: The person, or traveller on the quest has achieved control over the will, material, mental and emotional processes of human existence and his soul has become united with his Source. He is home.

Chapter 5

THE LESSER ARCANA
Meanings

Representing ENDEAVOUR, ENTERPRISE and PROGRESS. The worker — especially one who wants to get on with the job in hand or who is ambitious. Lower/modest income bracket.

Element: Fire.

Court Cards represent people (King, Queen, Knight and Knave)

KING OF BATONS

Upright:

An educated, mature man of strength, courage and staying power. He can see both sides of a problem or other people's points of view. Upholder of family traditions, loyal and friendly.

Reversed:
An intolerant man who lacks compassion for others. Dogmatic and fixed in outlook and ideas. Ruthless in ambitions and goals.

QUEEN OF BATONS

Upright:
A mature, practical woman who is devoted to her family and at the same time extends concern for community affairs and the environment. Has charm and personality and can act and think independently when necessary.

Reversed:
A possessive, overbearing woman. Capable of emotional blackmail and acting for her own ends. Has poor judgement. Quick to give and take offence.

KNIGHT OF BATONS

Upright:
A man who moves and acts swiftly. Has a very unpredictable but likeable manner. He brings change or alterations to plans — perhaps unexpected. He can organise something at the last minute and is generally fortunate.

Reversed:
A man who loves to argue and promotes trouble and conflict: a gossip. He brings unexpected change: he indicates difficulties with personal relationships — possible break-ups.

KNAVE OF BATONS

Upright:
A young man bringing good or interesting news. He has a reliable manner and is adaptable to any circumstances. A messenger or delivery boy. A young journalist or reporter.

Reversed:
A young man of dubious character: untrustworthy. His communications are misleading or exaggerated.

10 BATONS

Upright:
Powerful and fixed forces are operating in order to meet a deadline. An aggressive, blinkered approach which appears to be necessary, but perhaps this action could be re-assessed for its long-term value.

Reversed:
Deceptive influences are at work. Watch for misleading information designed to upset a situation.

9 BATONS

Upright:
All appears secure, but expect changes or opposition when courage and willpower are required. Your position is strong.

Reversed:
Delays and frustrations to plans and ideas. Need to compromise and adapt because of adverse conditions.

8 BATONS

Upright:
Favourable news or a journey is likely. Sudden opportunities and expected progress which need concentrated effort and initiative if you are to be successful.

Reversed:
Opportunities have been overlooked due to hasty action in the wrong direction. Need to re-examine ideas and actions.

7 BATONS

Upright:
Challenge and opposition to ideas and endeavours which will succeed providing you persevere. Any competition will be overcome.

Reversed:
Indecision and therefore loss of opportunity. Giving in to a challenge and failing to compete with conviction.

6 BATONS

Upright:
Good news regarding your hopes and wishes. Achievement is gained through hard work and careful, original planning.

Reversed:
Delays in your affairs and apprehension to the matter in hand and the people involved with it.

5 BATONS

Upright:
Struggle and strife which require all your tenancity and skill to overcome. Be prepared for obstacles and allow for alternative planning and ideas to get you through the present challenges.

Reversed:
Be prepared to negotiate your position, but beware that deception, misleading information and even fraud are possibilities in the background.

4 BATONS

Upright:
Success in career, work or profession due to your skill and hard work brings financial reward, contracts or agreements. Your social status is recognised and your position is established.

Reversed:
Lack of foresight. Insecurity and disharmony in your affairs. A need to be realistic where you should do some research into why things are not running smoothly. Re-route and re-plan ideas.

3 BATONS

Upright:
Success — rewards for enterprise and endeavour. Your dreams and plans come to fruition. Communications are successful.

Reversed:
Lack of balance in planning and communications. You have promised more than you can deliver. Unrealistic and impractical ideas and plans.

2 BATONS

Upright:
Your skill, courage and determination bring success and just rewards. Responsibilities are recognised and knowledge is attained through your creative and original actions which will bring benefits.

Reversed:
False optimism. Brief success resulting in disappointment. Unhealthy attitudes and motives with, perhaps, a desire for power at all costs. Your intentions need reassessing.

ACE OF BATONS: 1

Upright:
New beginnings: launching of new endeavours and enterprises. Allow intuition and originality to enhance your present plans which will lead to success.

Reversed:
Unexpected loss or frustration to plans. A lack of consideration and responsibility in your actions. Your present attitude shows lack of creativity. Nothing will be gained.

COINS

Representing both MATERIAL and FINANCIAL matters. Awareness to money, development and negotiation in business and for material gain. A sensitive and practical approach to life. Financiers, accountants, tradespeople.
Element: Earth.

KING OF COINS

Upright:
A capable, experienced, successful man. A businessman of character and intelligence. Loyal, trustworthy and devoted to those he loves and respects.

Reversed:
A materialistic, boring and unrefined man, out to make a 'quick buck'. Inflexible to self-improvement. Corrupt in financial dealings and a spendthrift.

QUEEN OF COINS

Upright:
A woman conveying prosperity and comfort. Supportive and sensitive to others' feelings. She has grace and a sense of occasion. Wealthy, but also generous to others.

Reversed:
An extravagant and overindulgent woman, of mean and narrow outlook. Uses wealth to manipulate others. An untrustworthy woman.

KNIGHT OF COINS

Upright:
A man who will defend and uphold tradition and justice. Mature outlook, responsible and both practical and conventional in his dealings.

Reversed:
A man who is set in his ways, rather boring and dogmatic. He suffers lack of foresight and is unable to initiate projects due to lack of imagination and vitality.

KNAVE (VALET) OF COINS

Upright:
A young, intelligent man — a student at university or college. A young businessman, keen to expand with new ideas and planning. Someone with application and diligence who will study and work in a responsible way.

Reversed:
An unintelligent, dull, boastful type of young man who is both unrealistic and illogical in his thinking and actions.

10 COINS

Upright:
Prosperity. Good news regarding money or material goods coming to you. Material security through family connections.

Reversed:

Possible financial loss through misfortune or poor investment. Restrictions to personal expansion. Loss of benefits through family circumstances.

9 COINS

Upright:

Accomplishment, material and social success. Ability to arrange, plan or manage financial affairs or a money matter.

Reversed:

Possible loss of friendship or a close contact. Theft of valuables. Financial matters are about to get out of hand.

8 COINS

Upright:

Successful use of your skills and craftsmanship which should be developed for future, long-term benefits.

Reversed:

Poor use of skills and lack of foresight and planning. Disillusionment. Likely to be susceptible to flattery which will lead to poor rewards.

7 COINS

Upright:

Financial or material progress can be made through hard work and originality. Money coming in from past endeavours.

Reversed:
Poor financial investment. Anxiety and financial difficulties due to past mismanagement of resources.

6 COINS

Upright:
Balance in money matters; gifts from and to others — generosity is working in all directions. Financial rewards.

Reversed:
Bad debts. Inability to repay loans. Loss of material security. Selfishness with resources.

5 COINS

Upright:
Financial difficulties in the not-too-distant future: perhaps unemployment or lack of proper financial reward. New opportunities and possibilities eventually forthcoming.

Reversed:
Need to be flexible in all things: ideas, projects and dealings with people. Use imagination and curb stubborness.

4 COINS

Upright:
Successful dealings in business matters and establishment of plans and structure. Financial rewards improve and stabilise. Good negotiations and agreements: legal documents especially favourable.

Reversed:
Inability to delegate will lead to problems in the future. Greed for power and material gain. Poor handling of finances.

3 COINS

Upright:
Success and progress in your financial/busines affairs. Any project requiring artistic skill and precision is favoured now and success will be forthcoming. Necessary help or assistance will support your endeavours.

Reversed:
Do not pursue that which is unnecessary. Unsuccessful in current projects and ideas, unless you listen, or seek sound advice. Money problems likely — pay attention to detail.

2 COINS

Upright:
Communications are likely to bring changes, journeys and new ventures which should be rewarding, stimulating and beneficial long-term as long as you pay attention to detail and small print.

Reversed:
Over-expansion, self-indulgence and an inability to 'follow through' projects. Details should be worked out carefully before commitment.

ACE OF COINS

Upright:
Wealth and material stability. Realisation and appreciation of life's comforts. Ability to make the best of what you've got for the time, confident that the law of supply and demand works for you.

Reversed:
Materialism: greed and acquisition, power and influence are too important in your scheme of things. Faith and vision are blocked out depriving you of a humanitarian outlook.

SWORDS

Representing MOVEMENT and PROGRESS for good or ill. Negotiation and DEBATE with skill and courage: COMMUNICATION. The LAW. Setting up of contracts/agreements. Executives, persons in authority.

Element: AIR.

KING OF SWORDS

Upright:

A man wo has original ideas and thinking, is rational and creative. Likes law and order and uses his authority. May not follow through his own ideas — likes to be in a position where others do this for him.

Reversed:

A calculating, impersonal character — rather oppressive, dangerous and sadistic.

QUEEN OF SWORDS

Upright:

A widow or a woman alone, intelligent, likes accuracy and gives attention to detail. She communicates well, but often brings bad news or gossip. Mentally alert.

Reversed:
Devious and deceitful, especially in promoting mis-understandings, perhaps for revenge. A dangerous woman who makes trouble.

KNIGHT OF SWORDS

Upright:
A highly skilled man who is unafraid of opposition and will act with foresight and courage. Bearer of news which could be controversial.

Reversed:
An impatient man who is ineffective and inclined to act impulsively, with a tendency to bite off more than he can chew.

KNAVE (VALET) OF SWORDS

Upright:
A messenger with diplomatic and negotiating skills, possibly bringing contracts, agreements or advice regarding details of small print in a document.

Reversed:
A young man who is devious, with skill at minding other people's business. Two-faced in his dealings and can symbolise the start of ill-health or bad news.

10 SWORDS

Upright:
Difficulties: conflict and sadness. There doesn't seem to be anything you can do about it, but take heart — things can only improve.

Reversed:

A temporary improvement which is helpful, but be warned — expect a deterioration in your affairs again soon.

9 SWORDS

Upright:

A disappointing period bringing unhappiness and anxiety. There is little you can do except bide your time and wait for the dust to settle. Justice seems to be lacking.

Reversed:

Beware of gossip or slander. A time when you feel isolated from others where doubts and suspicions prevail.

8 SWORDS

Upright:

Bad news — a crisis or calamity. A position in which you feel helpless. Don't give up hope — opportunities in other areas will bring renewed hope and purpose if you act promptly.

Reversed:

A mistake. Efforts made in the past bring no benefits at present. Depression and low spirits.

7 SWORDS

Upright:

Use planning, reason and logic and get your facts and figures right. Some opposition to your plans likely, so strengthen your position by being prepared and continue to persevere.

Reversed:
A likelihood of not finishing what you have started. Arguments. Make sure that any news or advice you have received is correct.

6 SWORDS

Upright:
A journey — short or long-distance. A circumstance which removes a problem (or a person) from your life for the time. Anxiety or worry is alleviated.

Reversed:
Expect difficulties to continue for the time.

5 SWORDS

Upright:
The outlook is becoming more clear, but you must deal with the present which will not go away on its own. Accept stalemate in a situation and prepare everything so you can move forward.

Reversed:
Beware of interference in your affairs. Hidden forces are at work which could bring some form of disaster to you.

4 SWORDS

Upright:
A break from routine or a difficult period with an opportunity to recharge your batteries.

Reversed:
Strength fails — depressing circumstances. A need to go back over old ground to find something lost or overlooked.

3 SWORDS

Upright:
Separation. Delays likely and some re-planning will be required; sorting out and discarding that which is unnecessary to make way for something new.

Reversed:
Quarrels. Body and mind out of balance. Need for new agreements to be negotiated or new contracts to be drawn up.

2 SWORDS

Upright:
Friendship and support are important at this time. Harmony and balance in all dealings.

Reversed:
Beware of misrepresentation. Unnecessary discord — someone is making trouble.

ACE OF SWORDS

Upright:
Strength and great determination brings success and prosperity.

Reversed:
Power used for the wrong reason. Injustice and unnecessary destruction prevails.

CUPS

Representing LOVE, HAPPINESS and JOY. Deep feelings. Humanitarian and religious or spiritual principles. Lawyer, businessman, religious/spiritual persons. Clergy. Persons in show business or cultural activities.
  Element: Water.

KING OF CUPS

Upright:
A professional man is at your disposal bringing help and advice which is a positive move in assisting you at this time. A solicitor or advisor is helping the matter.

Reversed:
Be aware of deception or dishonesty from a man. Injustice is likely and you are the loser. Watch your emotional reactions: try to keep control of your emotions in the face of difficulty.

QUEEN OF CUPS

Upright:
A fair-haired woman who is practical, loving and intuitive. Has a good imagination and is artistic and

creative. She is a good wife and mother or friend. Her manner can be rather 'dreamy' or sometimes pre-occupied.

Reversed:
Someone's word is unreliable. Beware of dishonesty in all your dealings. You cannot count on support from this woman.

KNIGHT OF CUPS

Upright:
An artistic, refined man is entering your circumstances who brings you a new idea, opportunity or invitation.

Reversed:
Beware of false agreements, deception, fraud or other distraction in your present affairs, from a man who gets carried away with impractical ideas, is cunning and scheming.

KNAVE (VALET) OF CUPS

Upright:
A young man, rather quiet, serious and studious in manner, who will help you by offering his services. He has common sense and good background knowledge.

Reversed:
Beware of someone professing real knowledge — perhaps a salesman with devious methods. There is flattery about designed to distract you.

10 CUPS

Upright:
Happiness, love, peace and harmony reigns. Good home conditions and environment.

Reversed:
Unexpected disruptions to normal routines. Unhappiness and discord around you. Are your motivations/intent for selfish reasons?

9 CUPS

Upright:
All is well. Emotions are stable, happiness and health are secure. Circumstances generate goodwill, optimism and generosity.

Reversed:
Sympathy and generosity has been misjudged or misplaced. Unhappiness and material loss.

8 CUPS

Upright:
A change of plans due to altered feelings. A new relationship promises to be deeper, bringing greater fulfillment. A delay in personal decisions.

Reversed:
Restlessness. Dissatisfaction: breaking off a relationship or abandoning present circumstances.

7 CUPS

Upright:
Beware of unrealistic thinking, illusions or daydreams in the present circumstances. Choose carefully, be practical taking all alternatives into account. Arrival at a sudden solution.

Reversed:
A goal is in sight. Self-deception. Beware of false information or a lost opportunity.

6 CUPS

Upright:
Memories of childhood or the past come up for review in some way. Links from the past renewed with helpful results.

Reversed:
Inability to cope with present circumstances, but the future looks brighter.

5 CUPS

Upright:
Unhappiness due to imperfect conditions around you — perhaps loss. Seek alternatives and renew old contacts. Be positive in the face of sorrow.

Reversed:
New ways of dealing with present circumstances. Meeting new people/new relationships which will eventually bring rewards.

4 CUPS

Upright:
You are taking things for granted. Emotional difficulties can bring disappointment unless you inject some enthusiasm into your ideas/projects/behaviour.

Reversed:
Beware excessive behaviour in social circumstances (over-eating, over-reacting), or of straining your body in some way.

3 CUPS

Upright:
The solving of a problem with satisfaction. Happiness and fulfillment all around you.

Reversed:
Delays and dissatisfaction. Self-indulgence can lead to uncontrollable circumstances arising.

2 CUPS

Upright:
Love. The coming together of two people, or it could be two ideas which bring satisfaction and co-operation. Emotional understanding and trust. Agreements signed.

Reversed:
Unsatisfactory relationship. Trust is betrayed. Separation. Opposition to plans and the breaking of agreements.

ACE OF CUPS

Upright:
Love, happiness, joy and plenty. The matter in hand will be fruitful.

Reversed:
Unhappiness. Loss of faith and trust. Love fails to save the situation at the moment. Dissatisfaction with a relationship.

INDEX

Ace 12
    Batons 105
    Coins 111
    Cups 122
    Swords 116
Air 13, 112
Astrol spread 22, 23, 34–40

Batons 12, 13, 100–5
    King 100–1
    Knave 102
    Knight 101
    Queen 101

Cavalier *see* Knight
Chalices *see* Cups
Chariot 29, 36, 61–2
Circular spread 22, 23
Clairvoyancy, developing 41
Coins 12, 13, 106–11
Conjurer 45–6
Court cards 12, 20
Cups 12, 13–14, 117–22
    King 117
    Knave 118
    Knight 118
    Queen 117–18

Death 30, 76–8
Decision-making process 40–1

Devil 27, 38, 81–3
Diviner 18

Earth 13, 106
Eight
    Batons 103
    Coins 108
    Cups 119
    Swords 114
Emperor 32, 52–4
Empress 50–1

Fire 13, 100
Five
    Batons 104
    Coins 109
    Cups 120
    Swords 37, 115
Fool 11, 39, 42–4
Fortitude 26–7, 71–3
Four
    Batons 104
    Coins 109–10
    Cups 121
    Swords 115–16

Greater Arcana 11–12, 14, 21
    examples of readings
        25–41
    interpreting 20, 42–99

Hanged Man 30, 31, 38, 74–5
Hermit 26, 65–7
High Priest 55–7
High Priestess 33–4, 47–9
House of God 84–6

Intuition 17, 40–1

Jester 42–4
Judgement 27, 29, 39, 95–7
Juggler 45–6
Junon 47–9
Jupiter 26, 55–7
Justice 38, 63–4

King 12, 13, 20
  Batons 100–1
  Coins 106
  Cups 117
  Swords 32, 37, 112
Knave 12, 13, 20
  Batons 102
  Coins 107
  Cups 118
  Swords 113
Knight 12, 13, 20
  Batons 101
  Coins 107
  Cups 118
  Swords 113

Lesser Arcana 12–14, 20
  examples of readings 31–41
  interpreting 100–22
Lovers 58–60

Magician 34, 45–6

Major Arcana see Greater Arcana
Minor Arcana see Lesser Arcana
Minstrel 45–6
Moon 89–91

Nine
  Batons 33, 102
  Coins 108
  Cups 119
  Swords 114

Page see Knave
Papess 47–9
Pope 55–7

Queen 12, 13, 20
  Batons 101
  Coins 106–7
  Cups 117–18
  Swords 112–13
Questioner 18
Questions, composing 15

Reading the cards 14–17
  decision-making process 40–1
  examples 25–41
Reine see Queen
Reversed cards 19, 29
Roi see King

Sceptres see Batons
Seven
  Batons 33, 37–8, 103
  Coins 108–9
  Cups 37, 120
  Swords 33, 114–15

Seven-card spread 18–20, 25–34
Shuffling 18, 20–1
Six
    Batons 103
    Coins 109
    Cups 120
    Swords 115
Star 87–8
Strength 71–3
Sun 92–4
Swords 12, 13, 112–16
    King 32, 37
    Knave 113
    Knight 113
    Queen 112–13

Temperance 30, 31, 38, 79–80
Ten
    Batons 102
    Coins 107–8
    Cups 119
    Swords 113–14

Three
    Batons 104–5
    Coins 110
    Cups 121
    Swords 116
Tower 84–6
Transformation 76–8
Twelve-card spread 20–4, 34–40
Two
    Batons 105
    Coins 110
    Cups 121
    Swords 116

Valet *see* Knave

Wands *see* Batons
Water 13–14, 117–22
Wheel of Fortune 26, 30, 36, 68–70
World 27, 30, 98–9

BIBLIOGRAPHY

Cooper, J.C.C., *An Illustrated Encyclopaedia of Traditional Symbols* (Thames & Hudson, 1978).

Douglas, Alfred, *The Tarot* (Penguin Books Ltd., 1974).

Haich, Elizabeth, *The Wisdom of the Tarot* translated by D.Q. Stephenson (Unwin Paperbacks, 1985).

Kaplan, S.R., *Tarot Cards for Fun and Fortune Telling* (Aquaria Press, 1978).

THE FAMILY MATTERS SERIES

Anniversary Celebrations   0 7063 6636 0
Baby's First Year   0 7063 6778 2
Baby's Names and Star Signs   0 7063 6801 0
Baby's Names   0 7063 6542 9
Barbecue Hints and Tips   0 7063 6893 2
Card Games   0 7063 6635 2
Card Games for One   0 7063 6747 2
Card Games for Two   0 0763 6907 6907 6
Card and Conjuring Tricks   0 7063 6811 8
Catering for a Wedding   0 7063 6953 X
Charades and Party Games   0 7063 6637 9
Children's Party Games   0 7063 6611 5
Common Ailments Cured Naturally   0 7063 6895 9
Does it Freeze?   0 7063 6960 2
Dreams and Their Meanings   0 7063 6802 9
Early Learning Games   0 7063 6771 5
First Time Father   0 7063 6952 1
How to be the Best Man   0 7063 6748 0
Microwave Tips and Timings   0 7063 6812 6
Modern Etiquette   0 7063 6641 7
Naming Baby   0 7063 5854 6
Palmistry   0 7063 6894 0
Preparing for Baby   0 7063 6883 5
Pressure Cooker Tips and Timings   0 7063 6908 4
Travel Games   0 7063 6643 3
Vegetarian Cooking Made Simple   0 7063 6941 6
Wedding Etiquette   0 7063 6868 1
Wedding Planner   0 7063 6867 3
Wedding Speeches and Toasts   0 7063 6642 5

VIIII

L'ERMITE